In Vitro
Laura Solomon
Proverse Hong Kong

IN VITRO is the debut poetry collection of prize-winning poet, Laura Solomon. It covers a wide range of topics:— the prophetess Pythia, England's Guy Fawkes, an alternative reality for New Zealand writer Janet Frame, earthquakes, in vitro experiments, spiders, tigers, vampire bats. The themes are universal. As Patricia Prime writes in *Takahē*, Laura Solomon is, "a tolerant, compassionate observer of nature and human nature. She is able to look into the lives, hearts and minds, not only of people, but of animals – using their thoughts and voices." Mainly written between 2003 and 2007 when the author was living in London, several of the poems have been placed in UK literary competitions and some have appeared in a number of international literary magazines, including *Aesthetica*, *Broadsheet*, *Frost Writing*, *Sentinel*, *The Shop*, *Landfall*, and *the London Poetry Festival Anthology*.

LAURA SOLOMON has a 2.1 degree in English Literature (Victoria University (New Zealand, 1997) and a Master's degree in Computer Science (University of London, UK, 2003).
She has won literary prizes in several competitions. She received a merit, in the Mere Literary Festival (UK: 2010); and was Runner Up, Edwin Morgan Poetry Competition (UK: 2009). She was commended in the Ware Poets Competition (UK: 2007) and the Essex Poetry Festival competition (UK: 2009). She was shortlisted in the Bridport Competition (UK: 2009) and her work appeared in the London poetry festival anthology (UK: 2009).
For her novella, *Instant Messages*, she was short-listed for the 2009 Virginia Prize and won the 2009 Proverse Prize.
She has had work accepted in the *Edinburgh Review* (UK) and *Wasafiri* (UK), *Takahe* (NZ) and *Landfall* (NZ). She has judged the *Sentinel Quarterly* Short Story Competition and the *Needle in the Hay* competition.
Her published works of fiction include: *Black Light*, *Nothing Lasting*, *Alternative Medicine*, *An Imitation of Life*, *Instant Messages*, *Hilary and David*, *The Shingle Bar Sea Monster and other Stories*, and *Vera Magpie*.

In Vitro

Laura Solomon

Proverse Hong Kong

In Vitro
by Laura Solomon.
Alternate 2nd revised edition published in Hong Kong
by Proverse Hong Kong February 2019
under exclusive right
ISBN 978-988-19935-6-4
2nd revised edition 1st published in Hong Kong by Proverse Hong
Kong, June 2014.
ISBN 978-988-19935-6-4

Copyright © Laura Solomon, June 2014.

First published in 2011 by HeadworX Publishers, Wellington, New
Zealand.

Enquiries to: Proverse Hong Kong, P.O. Box 259,
Tung Chung Post Office, Tung Chung, Lantau Island, NT,
Hong Kong SAR, China.
E: proverse@netvigator.com W: www.proversepublishing.com

The right of Laura Solomon to be identified as the author of this work
has been asserted by her
in accordance with the Copyright, Designs and Patents Act 1988.

Cover design by Artist Hong Kong Company and Proverse Hong Kong.

All rights reserved. No part of this publication may be reproduced, stored in a retrieval system, or transmitted, in any form or by any means, electronic, mechanical, photocopying, recording or otherwise, without the prior written permission of the publisher. The book is sold subject to the condition that it shall not, by way of trade or otherwise, be lent, re-sold, hired out or otherwise circulated without the publisher's prior written consent in any form of binding or cover other than that in which it is published and without a similar condition including this condition being imposed on the subsequent owner or purchaser. Please contact Proverse Hong Kong in writing, to request any and all permissions (including but not restricted to republishing, inclusion in anthologies, translation, reading, performance and use as set pieces in examinations and festivals).

British Library Cataloguing in Publication Data.
A catalogue record for this book is available from the
British Library.

Acknowledgements

Some of the poems in this collection first, and/or previously, appeared in the following publications:
Aesthetica (UK) (2007: Janet Frame is Lobotomised…); *Asparatus Magazine* (USA) (2010: Behind the Scenes at the British Museum); *Black Mail Press* (NZ) (2007: Ode to Mutt, The Misanthropic Magician, The Lion tamer's Lament, In Vitro, Closing Time in the Pub at the End of the Mind; 2009: The Marketplace); *broadsheet: new new zealand poetry* (NZ) (2010: Behind the Scenes in the Lost and Found at the British Museum, The Fix-it Man); *Coffee House Poetry* (UK) (2010: Blighty Wounds; 2012: Behind the Scenes in the Lost and Found at the British Museum); *Dawntreader* (UK) (2007: Tectonic); *Decanto* (UK) (2008: Blighty Wounds); *Delivered* (UK) (2007: In Bloom Mark II); *Dominion Post* (UK) (2011: The Fix-it Man); *Erbacce* (UK) (2010: You Will Know When You Leave); *Four Volts* (NZ) (2007: Halfway); *Frost Writing* (Sweden) (2009: In Vitro, Halfway); *Landfall* (NZ) (2008: Arachne Gets the Blues); *London Poetry Festival anthology* (UK) (2009: The Latest Lighthouse Keeper, You Will Know When You Leave); *Magazine* (NZ) (2007: The Vampire Bats…); molloy notebook blog (UK) (2011: In Shackles); *Ouroboros Review* (NZ) (2009: After Lights Out at the Horniman Museum); *Pirene's Fountain* (Australia) (2009: The Latest Lighthouse Keeper, Tectonic); *Sentinel* (UK) (2007: Closing Time in the Pub at the End of the Mind); *Ruminate Magazine* (USA) (2008: The Ghost of Roy Sullivan Laments, The Cartographer's Dream…); *Takahe T63* (NZ) (2008: Street Pet, In Bloom Mark II); *The Measure Magazine* (UK) (2007: You Will Know When You Leave); *The Shop* (Ireland) (2007: The Eternal Stupidity of the Wicker Man; 2008: In Bloom Mark II); Winged Ink blog (UK) (2011: Conversation Overheard on the Road to Salem).

Of the poems in this collection, the following have been well received in poetry competitions and festivals:
'The Latest Lighthouse Keeper' was commended in the Ware Poets Competition (UK, 2007) and also appeared in the London poetry festival anthology (UK, 2009); 'You Will Know When You Leave' was shortlisted in the Bridport Competition (UK, 2009) and also appeared in the London poetry festival anthology (UK, 2009); Pythia Gets the Blues was commended in the Essex Poetry Festival competition (UK, 2009).

Author's Acknowledgements
Grateful thanks to Roi Colbert, Raewyn Alexander and my family.

Contents

In Vitro	7
The Newcomer	10
Halfway	11
Ode to Mutt	13
Street Pet	15
The Misanthropic Magician	17
The Tiger Tamer's Lament	19
Arachne Gets the Blues	22
The Crows	23
The Vampire Bats – A Conversation	24
The Marketplace	26
After Lights Out at the Horniman Museum	27
Behind the Scenes in the Lost and Found at the British Museum	29
Tectonic	30
Janet Frame's Adversaries Have Their Way. Janet is Lobotomised and Spends Her Life Selling Hats in Oamaru	32
In Bloom Mark II	34
The Latest Lighthouse Keeper	36
Arrivals	37
Conversation Overheard on the Road to Salem	38
Pythia Gets the Blues	39
In Shackles	40
Blighty Wounds	41
Closing Time in the Pub at the End of the Mind	42
The Poet Leaves the Table	44
The Eternal Stupidity of the Wicker Man	46
The Fix-It Man	47
The Cartographer's Trauma Upon Waking	48
The Ghost of Roy Sullivan Laments	49
Guy Fawkes Gives His Sincerest Apologies	51
Sunday Evening, Driving West	52
You Will Know When You Leave	54
Notes	55

From Reviews of the first edition of *In Vitro*	56
The Proverse Prize and Author's portrait	57

In Vitro

My children are made by me, but borne by others.
The pain of childbirth holds no appeal; the screeching, the
tearing, the blood,
the whole world drowned in amniotic fluid. A flood.
The subsequent stitches of brightly coloured thread.

How infinitely preferable to breed them in a petri dish,
pinch of you, grain of me, eye of something-or-other – *behold*,
the mighty zygote.
Nothing is left to chance, I plan it all according to the law that I
was handed down.
Aim, Method, Results, Conclusion – a fourth form experiment of
sorts.

You can call me clinical, I don't care. I don't believe in accidents.
Fate is for fools.
My pristine white coat, my catheter of silicone, the blank white
walls of the lab;
these instruments of creation are all I've ever known.

This is the way a world begins – manufactured in a room where
there are no seasons.

There is not one mother, but many.
Fresh girls are a dime a dozen in this neck of the woods.
Where do they come from? I hear you ask. *Your steady little
supply.*
Please, allow me to reply. These girls are found all over.
Some I discover out on the street, perched in doorways or gutters,
some advertise in the local paper, 'Womb For Rent', in bold
black type,
some I kidnap in broad daylight or by the pale glare of the moon.
Slave trade.

Some girls are cheaper than others.

One by one, they climb onto my table. I plant those little lives.

I monitor the mothers, pump them full of fish oils, vitamins, milk,
snatch cigarettes from their mouths, take the vodka from their
hands.
"Mind how you go," I say. "You girls need to be careful now.
Enough of your skylarking."
I poke and prod and scan. All goes according to plan.

"A splendid diagnosis," I solemnly declare, with voice pitched
low to hide my fear.

Once the cells are implanted, I chart their progress, watch them
grow.
I tend to them as you would to a garden,
count up the weeks in staggered steps, a rocket launch in reverse.
There are important milestones. For instance –
week six, when the hearts start up and the tadpole tails shrink.
The vanishing reminder of our amphibian roots.
Week seven, when they sprout spinal cords and brains.
A branching nervous system. They are not yet old enough to feel
pain.
They will learn to tell the difference between dark and light
and at week thirty-nine they are ready for life.

They could be born at any time.

When I am least prepared, they arrive,
a great rush – multiple mothers, multiple births,
in a gush the waters break –
an army of them, all up and down the hospital ward,
all lungs fill with air,
the shout goes out, a unanimous cry,
as myriad tiny eyes see daylight for the first time.

Somewhere, something shatters. A pane.
And so the future is born.

I give them no names.
I hawk them for profit, sell them on.
If you're cunning you can make quite a mark-up.
I never said I wasn't mercenary.

"How heartless," you say, "how cut-throat, to give what was yours away."
You're oblivious to the fact that selling isn't giving.
You don't know where to draw the line.

How can you say that what I do is wrong?
To whom do they belong?
To no-one. They were never mine.

The Newcomer

Let's just say it crawled across the snow.
No. This waiting's situational.

In the nursery we've prepared the ABC blanket,
the walls have been painted a saintly white,
we've got the rattle, the dummy, the cot.
We expect not what is, but what is not.
The mobiles hang from the ceiling,
glinting in the treacherous light of morning.
Brightly coloured shapes –
something at which the baby can stare.

We pretend not to care that it's weeks overdue.
No-one's inducing anything.

Brought forth by force it would never learn to walk,
but would fall flat on its face,
like a cardboard doll when you yank away its prop.

Any day now, you say, any day now,
our little darling will arrive.

It's all right for *you*
you're not the one lugging this basketball around,
this feeder, this leech, this human parasite.

I stagger from room to room, barely alive.

Halfway

Nobody knows the nature of the thing.
For weeks it has sat in its jar, reeking not of life or death but of both.
Something in between.
It has the beginnings of a tail, two legs; a distinctly primordial air.
Eyes as dark as black holes peer out at the world. Anti-suns.

This morning we sat at the breakfast table, nothing much to say,
until you thought it wise to mention the war in Iraq –
you knew my brother was fighting there and you wanted some kind of reaction.
As a scientist with electrodes prods at a frog to see what twitches.
Nothing moved – my face remained as blank as a sheet of paper.
Decades ago I trained myself not to react to you.

All last night the baby cried – an incessant wail reminiscent of sirens.
The door to its room was left ajar – but no-one moved to comfort it;
I thought it your turn, you thought it mine,
Lord, pity the child born to those who walk the line!
You wept for the kid when you awoke, but I thought *crocodile tears*.

This afternoon I stumbled across a basket full of washing,
that you'd abandoned halfway to the line.
Shirts and sheets spilled every which way,
but you could not tell me when I asked,
what on earth could have occurred to interrupt such a vital, terrible task?

The railway line that runs down the back of our house never was completed.
You tried to tell me that they ran out of track, but I knew that to be a blatant lie.
It was you who called a halt to proceedings –
phoned up British Rail and begged them not to continue. Such is your way.

This chessboard that you forced me to walk away from,
hangs suspended in midair (there are wires but they are invisible).

You seem to have the feeling that you've won,
captured my queen and Lord only knows what else,
but I know the truth to be closer to some unholy eternal
stalemate.
That grin's a Cheshire's grin. When it's God v the Devil, no-one
loses, no-one wins.

Ode to Mutt

Nobody, Laika, captured their imagination like you.
So many arrived before me, honouring you with their words,
that I hardly know what to say.
They're paying me, Laika, to make this speech. I am employed.
The ghost of you must be sick of it by now; the poems, the tales,
the odd shrieking song –
The yapping of ten thousand dogs trapped in ten thousand
kennels.
So tedious to have become myth, when all you really want is
silence, peace.
To quietly orbit the orbiting earth.

And what of the other dogs, the ones they passed over, in favour
of you?
The mutts that went on to lead full and happy lives;
salivating, biting, yelping, humping the legs of humans and
tables.
Were they envious or grateful? Did they want to take your place?
What did you have anyway, that made you so special?
Nothing. You were doomed to immortality. It was your fate. You
were the one.

It was as if a part of everybody had been sent into space with you.
You carried our hopes for the future, for what could be achieved.
They wanted to monitor your blood pressure, your heart rate,
your breathing,
to see how the rest of us would fare, if we followed in your path.
You were their experiment – they wired you up.
They wanted to know how deeply you slept, and if you dreamed.

You were a Jesus of a dog. We all knew it. Your harness was
your cross.
So? I can hear your shrug in your bark. *What about it?*

You were always nonchalant.

There had been others before you;
your comrades, Albina and Tsyganka – a few sacrificial mice.
But they were merely suborbital.

You burst straight through to the other side
and saw, for a moment, it all;
the diamond stars, the distant galaxies, so many glistening
moons.

The universe pulsed in your veins. Time stalled, spluttered,
stopped.
You were shot straight out of the cannon of history – fired into
eternity.
It was the sun that killed you, cooked you alive;
fried your fur, charred your bones, scorched your skin.
Your eyeballs sizzled in your skull as your last bitter bark
reverberated in space.
And seemed as if it might echo forever.

The tender howl of betrayal.

No-one knows how long you took to die – the Russians claimed,
for years, it was a week
but now, it transpires, you were baked within hours.
Could you tell us the exact time, let us know?

Laika, friend, enemy, are you out there somewhere –
your skeleton still in orbit, your dream a universal dream?

Only you know the truth and you are gone and can never tell.
You have become metaphor. Such is your wish.

Still, the curious in our number cannot help but wonder –
if you were here now amongst us and given human voice
what would you have to say? And who would listen?

Street Pet

It was the neighbour who first mentioned him.
I had locked myself out, a typical trick.
I am absent-minded at best – at worst, not all there.
I had doors to rap upon, fences to climb.
They seemed impossibly high.
I'd left a window open out back – a possible entrance point.
Number 31 weren't home; so I tried the other side – 35.
It was the first time that we'd met.
I explained my situation – talk soon turned to the new street pet.
Have you seen him, the fox? Just this month, he's begun to appear.
Yes, I said, at dusk.
And the coat on him. Not a spot of mange. A gorgeous shade of rust.

I was familiar with the fellow he spoke of –
Mr Vulpes has the same look as all his urban kindred,
his space encroached upon time and again,
he's furtive, scurrying across the road with a wary, world-weary air.
He's seen too many of his cousins mowed down.
He knows a thing or two about headlights.
We took a step outside. What glories greeted my eyes!
But your garden! It's amazing. The borders so neat. A place for everything and everything in its place.
O, it takes no time at all, once the ground work is done.
My neighbour, you see – he's learned the value of humility.
You should see ours, I muttered. *Waist high weeds. Unmanageable.*

Our two gardens, side by side – his all order, mine all chaos.
That towering fence – how would I ever get across?
So few gaps, no cross beams. Nowhere to set your feet.
The fox manages it, said my neighbour. *Have you seen?*
On the street, yes. But never leaping fences. Never doing that.
You'd be amazed, came the reply. *Necessity does as necessity demands.*
(Pause)
I have a ladder if you need it.

Pig-headed, I said, *I'll be fine.*
Within two minutes I was stuck – snared, like a thing in a trap.
Laughable, a clown.
Something was hooked somewhere.
Here, he said –
and with one swift movement swung the ladder across, helped me over, down.
From my side I smiled and waved in gratitude and mortification –
nothing to say for myself, I climbed in through my own bathroom window.

There have been other fences, other times too numerous to mention.
I shall keep Mum about those.
Last night I saw him again, that fox.
Head down, headed for elsewhere.
He moves as if no-one can see or hear him.
He never meets your eye. He knows much better than that.

From time to time we pass on the street,
my orderly neighbour and I – we wave;
sharp in his mind, God knows what;
the knowledge in mine of the fences I climbed
and the others I faltered at.
Though forced, I took them all in the end;
a deaf mute learning to speak,
Helen Keller learning colours –
a cripple beginning to dance.

The Misanthropic Magician

Christ, what do you want now – another bunny?
This old top hat has an endless supply,
though most of these leporids do not leap anywhere,
rather they flop, half-dead, to the floor. Still you want more.

Wait; it gets worse.

My assistants always leave through the first exit door,
claiming maltreatment, foul language, abuse;
their outfits stay with me, are mine –
the sparkling vests, the star-studded knickers, the ruby-coloured heels,
with these beneath my pillow I do sleep. And never dream.

I keep their clothing; I forget their names.
My secret source of shame – some of these girls really were
sawn in half,
by accident, though some claim by design.

In honour of their memory, well I'm pining all the time.

Then there was that business with the water into wine.
"Cheap trick," they said. "These cups can be bought for £1.99
from any third-rate joke store."
"You're right," said I. "I'm a fake, I'm a fraud – a foul and filthy whore."

You should know better yet you still want more.

There have been other girls, undone by blades,
by my knives that failed to fly true;
that stuck into faces and wrists and thighs –
stuck deep in the heart of you.

O, the scandal! I could've died.

Instead, I fled – town to town, station to station;
they could never leave me be, always wanted information.
With my noontime squint, my midnight swagger,
my smashed wristwatch, the cloak, the dagger –
"Where did you come from? Where will you go?"
It was nearly, but not quite, more than I could handle.

Infamy became my mantle. I guess you could say it was a
vanishing of sorts.

But still, unsatisfied, you say you want more.

In the end, I sought refuge on the stage –
like the girls, like the green rooms, they all seem the same;
the lights, too hot, too bright, the anonymous faces in the cheap
seats, in the gods –
the invisible wall that separates you from me. A divide.

This hall could be anywhere; in a foreign city, or some strange
town,
or pinned way out on the rim of space. Butterfly style.

From the rear of the hall I hear you call, "The universe must
have its way."
And I know that I could give you exactly what you need,
if only I wasn't quite so hard of hearing,
a little more bullet-proof, a little more daring –
if I could only make this circle perfect, and just for once,
stop myself from disappearing.

The Tiger Tamer's Lament

They told me that it would be easy. They lied.

To the interview I wore my best black suit, a veiled hat.
I sat with my feet pressed tightly together, hands folded in my lap.
Like a mourner at a funeral.

"Piece of cake," they said. "They're pussycats, really. Obedient, not wild."
They smiled like crocodiles.
"One flick of the whip and they sit. They'll perch on chairs if you crack the thing twice.
If you want to make them dance with you, just snap your fingers thrice."

They made it sound like a recipe. Fail safe. Idiot proof. A miniscule risk, at most.

First day on the job,
I discovered that the guy employed before me had been brutally mauled.
It was one of the acrobats who whispered it in my ear;
she followed me into the ladies' room and hissed,
He didn't make it. He languished in hospital for three long weeks before giving up the ghost.

They'd thought for an instant that he might pull through,
but more than bones had been broken.
More than blood had been lost.

Beware, she said. *It's unnatural. To make such creatures pets. There are ramifications.*
And I wondered what she meant by that.

But for me there was to be no backing out. I had signed the dotted line.
In my tight white suit, I stepped bravely into the ring.
It was only a rehearsal, but it felt like the real thing.

A mother and her son faced me. "Here kitty, kitty," I called,
sweet, soft and low.
I eyed them and they eyed me. Part of me was already waiting
for the blow.

How to explain to these animals that ever since childhood this
had been my dream?
To enter the ring and have them kneel, tuck their claws into their
fur,
cease, for a moment, their incessant snarling, lay their muzzles in
my lap. Purr.

But we did not understand one another, those tigers and I –
the gap between us was as unbridgeable as that between sea and
sky.

I didn't speak their language, nor did they speak mine. I was no
Mabel Stark.
"Make sure you show 'em who's master," the boss had said.
"Keep calm, don't lose your head."

I cracked the whip. Nothing. I gave it another snap. The mother
pounced.
The pain split my mind in two. It's true that I may have blacked
out,
but in the instant before I fell to the floor,
I saw my own face reflected in that tiger's golden eye.

That was the first occasion. I recovered. It took a while.
"No more time for rehearsals," the ring-master cried. Suddenly
the act was live.

I was determined not to lose. I used my whip with abandon, I
kept them at bay.
"Sit," I yelled and they obeyed.
You could see the resentment, the anger, in their eyes.
It blazed like some kind of fire. They did not prance.

The third time I got them up onto chairs. I felt quite victorious
until a spectator yelled,
"It all comes to nothing if there's no dance. What kind of act is
this? Get outta here man, quit taking the piss."

And so we learned to waltz, not by choice but through necessity,
a graceless two-four affair.
The act lacked flair.
More a shuffle than a dance,
though once I thought I heard somebody say,
that if you held your head that way, just right, and half-closed
your eyes,
and squinted into the light,
that when I waltzed with the son,
you could almost imagine (had you half a mind to) that he and I
were one.

Whichever way you look at it, we have reached an uneasy truce.
Each has marked the other – whip cuts hide;
I do not walk naked. I wear long trousers, polo-neck sweaters,
scarves.
(You have to look beneath if you want to see the scars.)

Arachne Gets the Blues

The webs, the webs, always with the webs.
Surely there's more to existence than this sticky little thread
that strings from tree to tree like some heavenly rope
we can never swing by.

Food is the point, the hunt is everything to ladies like me,
I used to enjoy it, the struggling of the prey –
the pitiful attempts to break free.
I guess you could say that it gave me a kick.
Now I feel nothing at all.

Well look at that, I say with a shrug, *another sucker, trapped.*
Some of these flies really ought to look where they're going.
What's the point in having all those eyes if you don't know how to use them?
You'd think they'd try to learn from the mistakes of those who went before,
but they pay no heed to their ancestors. To their demise.

Same old, same old – the brutal struggle, the fight to break free,
until they, like me, resign. It's only ever a question of time.
Everybody's just going through the motions.
Still, when all's said and done, I'd rather be on our side than theirs.
Who wouldn't, given the choice?

It's all fairly painless. I like to keep the suffering to a minimum;
just *chomp, one, two* and it's over. Done and dusted.

This afternoon, in a backyard filled with ordinary angels,
as I sink my glistening fangs into another black and twisting body,
it strikes me, and not for the first time, that this is nothing more than role play,
that this tree is only a stage; that I must have something better to do.

The Crows

The highest branch is reserved.
It's our special place. It has our names on it.
We perch there silently, feigning nonchalance.
Out of reach of cats and other creatures
that might fancy us as prey.

Far below us, tabbies roam.
They snack on mice – drag them inside,
lay them out on the dining room floor, like snacks,
entrails splayed. An offering to a god long departed.
You look at me, I look at you;
eyes speak without words – *that could've been us.*
Tasty morsels.

Although small (little more than kittens, really) they're ruthless,
those moggies –
they hide in the long grass, waiting to leap,
paying little mind to mother's warnings – be cautious!
They know better – a gloved cat catches no mice.
Pounce and be damned.

Every now and then, we dare to take to the sky in flight;
it's boredom that drives us to it.
We pull a few half-hearted acrobatics hoping to please
somebody;
but nobody watches, not even the cats – you see, there's just us
two.

Wing-tip to wing-tip, it's choreographed by us,
we spend hours rehearsing our mangled stunts.
Nothing is signed with our honour.

To our favourite branch we return.
This tree holds every sort of weather;
you claim that the wind has unsettled your feathers.
I say, *I don't see why I should care.*

You always were the more vainglorious of the pair.

The Vampire Bats – A Conversation

It's never easy. It would have been so much better to be
nothing more than ordinary.

Why us? Why were we chosen when others were overlooked?
It seems so *unlikely*. We are something we never asked to be.

There's rivalry – *my fangs are bigger than your fangs*.
Fights about the length of wingspan. Who has the bigger talons;
petty issues.
The great amongst us act as if they've somehow risen above –
the lesser scrap it out.

I guess you could say we are a clan – a mafia of sorts; less
forgiving.
We have secret plans, hidden glands.

Mice are for the other buggers – the wimps who don't know how
to really bite.
Insects, pollen, frogs – such titbits are not for us. We prefer the
human stuff.

Blood will have blood.

We have time on our hands. Time and again,
we summon the guts to take to the sky and spin
one more slowly swooping circle around that old oak tree.

Weary, we cling to the highest branch,
hang upside down for a spell, wings beating the empty air,
biding time, preparing for take-off.

There are choices to make –
when to lay low, when to swoop and strike;
how deep to sink the teeth.

There's the puncture site to consider –
whether it's best to hit ankle, wrist or neck.
Swift, correct decisions can be the difference
between famine or feast.

On dark nights you'll find us, beneath the treacherous gleaming moon,
tapping the tip of one canvas-like wing against your windowsill as you sleep,
testing all your locks. Checking to see what has been securely bolted.
Discovering what has not.

There's an army of us now – any day soon we'll smash the pane.
We're just biding our time. We are *The Lost Boys* born again.
We have nothing to lose and everything to gain.

Brace yourself children –
those 747s outside the airport just *look* like they're going nowhere.
We're used to the gaze, the public glare. It makes no difference to us.

We had no choice but to learn how to fly –
our wings make noise like distant thunder, or else a distant sigh.

Did I hear somebody say, some time tomorrow or yesterday –
the chosen eat the feeble. The forgotten few will rise again;
the chosen chomp through everything. *The chosen eat the feeble.*

And blood, my friends, will have blood.

The Marketplace

Everything is for sale here.

Beef jerky, birds in wicker cages, baseball bats;
hand in hand, the two of us stride the aisle –
you pointing out what I might like to purchase,
me smiling and turning away.

Snakes, salami, salamanders,
unidentifiable items in cages –
things that cannot be named.
A cacophony of sound, the birds, the frogs, ringing in my ears.

Nothing is for free here.

I reach one hand into my purse
empty-handed, I turn to you,
but you say, *don't have nothing for you.*

The noise is deafening.

After Lights Out at the Horniman Museum

We only look dead. When the lights go out
(and after the cleaning lady has been and gone)
you see the other side of the story.
It's only been an act all along. We spring to life –
like nursery toys were once purported to do.

The dodo yawns and snaps his beak.
The moths and the butterflies leap from their pins,
careful not to damage their fragile wings.
The beetles clack. Nobody makes a song and dance.
We've been in Blighty long enough – we know better.
We're local now. Nobody smashes panes –
though it's rumoured that one of the more melodramatic eagles
threw a hissy fit last Friday and threatened to shove a wing
through the glass.
The remnants of decorum held him back. A severed pride.

Most of the rest of us are bitterly resigned – we exist to be
displayed.
Glassy-eyed hostages.
We're years past asking –
which side of the glass are you (*stammer*) which side are you on?
We understand the rules – *just act happy*.
You get a few thickos, dumb bunnies,
stick-in-the-muds who refuse to play along.

The merman could be one;
still bitching about being excluded from The Great Exhibition.
He always was big-headed. Dissatisfied with his position and his
place
relegated to that dank side room, with the African tribal masks
and those ridiculous glass cages filled with tiny stuffed birds
perched too gaily on twigs. Ideas above his station.
He wants centre stage. Reception area.
Silly bugger's still claiming to be the real thing
decades (nay, centuries) after it's been proven that he's a fake.

Us underlings – we know who we are –
this precious night is all we have.
We rustle for hours in the dark, grateful not to be watched until
the first key of the day turns in the lock.

Quick quick quick – assume natural pose.

**Behind the Scenes in the Lost and Found
at the British Museum**

Why can't these people be more careful?
How tricky can it be to keep track of your possessions?
If I didn't know better, I'd think they bought just to lose.
I never misplaced a thing. I am the perfect warden. A keeper, of
sorts.

To the left of that stack over there to the right –
somebody's red mittens, somebody else's red shoes.
Rarely do I give them what they ask for,
even if what they think is lost has been found.

I rummage in piles. I take my time.
I return to the counter empty-handed.
"Sorry," I say. "Don't have nothing for you."
I hold out my hands, palms upwards. A universe of vacancy.

Their faces hold worlds of disappointment. I pretend that I care.
I never let on that something isn't right.

The beehive glass of the Great Court lets in far too much light.

Tectonic

This country rests on two great plates. It's they that produce the instability
and also the fun stuff – geysers, hot pools, volcanoes. The land never sleeps.
My grandfather looks out the window and says,
Let's never forget that terrible earthquake that devastated Napier back in '31.
Everything gone. The insurance blokes called it an 'act of God', which failed to wash with the non-believers, who blamed it on the world.
Were there warnings, were there signs – a stillness in the air?
Did the birds freeze in mid-song? Did the animals act strangely?

Crisis after crisis – a litany of tragedies. Or else, improvisation.
Lampposts invented new angles. On the band rotunda, the clock hands stuck,
forever 10.47am – the time the earthquake struck. Everything did something;
gas pipes broke, power lines snapped, harbour walls buckled, roads split open wide, railway lines twisted.
Nothing so out of the ordinary –
just the earth running through its checklist, ticking boxes.
The dust rose, and then settled. Just in time for the fire.
It swept through, a wave of flame.
Unfortunates were trapped beneath beams.
Doctors rushed forward, morphine in hand –
soon the captured felt no pain. Cliffs fell.

Some spent the night in the open air.
Kind people in nearby towns opened up their homes.
Most hotels were destroyed –
the Masonic collapsed completely, a wall at the Empire crumbled,
leaving the rooms on one side exposed. Guests awoke – looked out into empty space,
fresh vacancy in their eyes. They'd lost their city, a lovely one.

But my, O my, with what fortitude, what resilience,
what purpose of mind, they rebuilt the place.
All that glorious Art Deco. Decorated stucco.
Street by street, wall by wall, up it went;
the best architects were shipped down from the big smoke,
to plot and plan and design.
There was a carnival of sorts – the city was declared 'reborn'.
Citizens threw their hands in the air and rejoiced. They had been
given new land.
The sea had retreated for good. After all, no great disaster.
Like all endings, it was also a beginning.
The city that had been faded in their minds.
(The art of forgetting isn't hard to master.)

The plates continue their treacherous work – no, they are not to
be trusted.
They shift beneath like restless children that refuse to go to bed –
*There's fun stuff on TV – let's stay up, wreak havoc, spread
dread.*

My grandfather looks out the window, takes in the wisp of
smoke, says –
They say Rangitoto's going to blow.
And though nobody can predict the exact hour when the thing
will go,
they say, *any day now, any day now* – when it happens you will
know.

Janet Frame's Adversaries Have Their Way.
Janet is Lobotomised and Spends Her Life Selling Hats in Oamaru.

What good would she have been anyway,
left the way she was, full of dotty ideas, half-crippled by madness?
There're enough raving lunatics in the world,
we don't need one more curly-haired crazy,
lolloping about the streets, spilling prophecy.

What good would she have been anyway,
claiming to be from her Kingdom by the Sea,
perching on gravestones in the Otago Cemetery,
staring into the far distance,
like somebody who could see something we couldn't?

And see her there, so happy, all her pain chopped out, eradicated,
along with all her brilliance. Smiling, always smiling – so what
if the eyes look dead?

It's not visionaries the world needs, but hat sellers.

She was something that could not blend in,
too many sharp angles, too many gaudy colours,
and gawd that hair,
but anything, you'll find, can be reduced to black and white,
anything can be shoved into a box,
it's just a question of how much has to be chopped off
in order to get it to fit.

After all, anybody can write a book. It's retail work that's tricky,
all those numbers to add up and subtract,
when you tally up at the end of the day (that's if they choose to
grant you such power),
all those hats to keep in those tidy little piles,
same colours, same shapes, all together, all neat,
a place for everything. Everything in its place.

All those people to so faithfully serve.

Don't ask me who made the mould – somebody else, a long,
long time ago.
Who cares now, when that thing was created, or how?
we all managed to squeeze ourselves into it,
so why shouldn't she be forced to do the same?

Who cares what she could've or would've achieved,
left to her own devices?

The important thing is that we maimed her while we had the
chance,
before she grew too big for the boots we wanted her in.

O please now, children, don't make a fuss,
She could've been one of the greats, they said,
now she's one of us.

In Bloom Mark II

I'm not the first to pass this way, nor will I be the last.
There has been a not-so-stately procession of us,
taking time out from the world.
Empires may well have crumpled while I was watching some unnamed insect,
steady and determined, work its way from A to B.

We are the oblivious, cripples craving oblivion.
Failing that, we find solace in small glories;
some limp glumly past the magnolias –
exclaiming as to their loveliness,
others, speech beyond them,
gurgle and point at the peonies.
Those of a Wordsworthian bent observe the daffodils.
They wither and wilt on the windowsills.
So transitory. Nothing lasts forever.
The mind filters what it will.

Some avert their eyes from all beauty.
They see only the white room of the present; the chair, the table, the lamp,
the bed with its stiffly starched sheets –
ghosts, wolves, vampires – apparitions conjured from the deep.
We are the ones who've been across the river.
O, what stories we could tell. We have our own special language;
code words for hell.
Some things can never be called by their real names.
How was the trip for you, my sweet?
Did you forget to pay the ferryman? Or did you pay him twice?
Darling, don't even *think* about the price.

The nurses come and go.
I suspect them of snickering, but I can't prove anything.
They have the upper hand. We are at their mercy.
I remember their faces; I forget their names.
At noon, somebody points to the orb that hangs suspended in the sky and says,
"Bella Luna." So bright, so quiet, so meaningless.
At midnight, a nod at the clock, "It's lunchtime now, dear."

I say nothing of note – Lord knows, it's always four a.m. here.
I am going to meet you over there.
All is not lost. There are always the blooms.
Everybody has favourites;
for their blood red skirts, bulbous, silken,
it's the tulips that I adore.
And the poppies for what they signify –
soldiers lost in some never forgotten war.

The Latest Lighthouse Keeper

The lamp no longer shines. It's been disconnected since time immemorial. Cut off.
This place has been long abandoned. Only an idiot would take up residence here.
We choose, of course. We are not forced.

There could've been another way.
Rust coats my stained fingers as I climb the iron stairs.
Some come for the view – me, I'm here for the ghosts.

On this first night, at midnight they show up;
as predictable as clichés – the pale ones in billowing white nightgowns,
the multi-coloured guys – green, purple with green rings, green with yellow rings,
any combination, in fact, of ring and base colour, you might care to dream up.

So strange. The lovely ancient lace, browning now at the edges,
the beads that hem the garments. The fancier ones sport feathers.

They are from all the centuries. They come marching in, like saints –
an invisible orchestra keeps the beat. Ghostly music enchants the air –
like the scent of flowers from some other-worldly garden.

Anybody else would run screaming.
Me, I keep very silent. Me, I keep very still.
I have always loved a parade.

This is the most excitement I've had in decades.

Even before they depart, I'm down on my knees, praying, saying,
O when will you return?

But they have other visits to make –
it's over, now, my turn.

Arrivals

Way past midnight they commence their march.
To lock the door against them does no good –
they are not restrained by something as simple as ordinary wood.

They have minds of their own. They do as they like – oblivious to my presence.
They do not hurry – they potter lazily, unconcerned by the natural order of things.
I wait for them to leave, like someone condemned to act accordingly.
They do not know their place; nor I mine. Some things belong nowhere at all.
There is no notion of hierarchy for creatures such as this. O hellish bliss!

It would do no good to stand and stare.
I look the other way, pretending (too hard) not to care.

Conversation Overheard on the Road to Salem

Think you're so fancy in that pointy hat,
with the audacity to just *assume* your black floating cape is the best.
Those warts are only stick-on, m'dear.
I can see right through you.

Those newts you keep in jars, gloating of their powers,
are just as plastic as dolls.
Pathologically competitive, that's your problem –
if I've told you once, I've told you a thousand times.
Pretending you know how to walk the line,
you're barely balancing as we ease on down this road.

Still, for all my bitching, we're on the same side,
we'll hold onto each other when the deal goes down –
you pretend to float and I'll pretend to drown.

Pythia Gets the Blues

God, why do I always have to tell you the truth?

High on snake fumes, eyes rolled back in my head,
head full of fire, prophesy flaming on my tongue,
you consult me on everything from
the personal to the political.
Imagine the responsibility!
What if I get it wrong?
You expect my advice
before going to war, before founding colonies,
before planting your fields,
before proposing to your beloved.

And what do I get in return?
A kick in the head if I'm lucky.

And all those eyes, watching, always watching.
Too many of them, trained on me.

Lying that I'm living beneath my dignity.
I did not ask for it – you put me here.

Take them then, these words,
burning spheres in my hands.

Fires flicker and die in my eyes.

In Shackles

There must be some way out of this.
Iron cuts my wrists.
Around one ankle, a ball and chain.

I have been sitting here since the last ice age.
Nobody guesses how old I am.

They think one, maybe two hundred years;
my hair matts, my fingernails twist, gnarled –
my eyes roll back in my head,
a leper imitating prophesy.

For five quid, I'll tell you your future.
You may not like what you hear.

O my dear, I will tell you the truth.

I am out of time. I don't think, I just do.

Like the sun, I burn;
sparks fly from the fire at my feet,
what care I about these chains,
I don't mind this servitude –
spitting, hissing like Caliban,
formulating, for *centuries*, escape plans.

The law was handed down.
Join forces underground.

Go on, spit in my eye and I'll tell you your future;
you'll die, I will never grow old.

Blighty Wounds

We are the ones who refused to go 'over the top',
choosing instead the coward's route. The closest exit door.

Ardent for relief, we swapped the flicker of death
and the faint hope of glory,
for the promise of certain pain.

I'll be some use to them as a cripple, but none at all dead!
The old refrain.
I am starving here, and so are they at home, we may as well starve together.
All the lies we fed ourselves. The constant drizzling rain.

The rats, the filth, the mud, the cold. Entire days with no sleep.
The rat-a-tat-tat of machine gun fire.
Enough to drive the strongest of strong minds insane.
No food – the gaping hole in the stomach that mimics the black hole in the chest;
constant enemy fire from shells, machine-gun, rifle and gas.

Some put a bullet through the foot; some (more dramatically)
shot a shell into the brain.
Some spoke of the shamelessness, most spoke of the shame.

Better that, we thought, than to be like our counterparts –
shipped home in body bags, without labels, without names.

Returned, we are ghosts of men, marked.
Forever set apart – never the same way again.
Avoiding each others' eyes, hair covered.
Smiles set rigid like masks – attempting to blend into the fray;
little scores of Kaiser Sozes. It's the limp that gives us away.

Closing Time in the Pub at the End of the Mind

We are the dregs. We are what's left over when all the sane, the normal people,
the people who instinctively know how to keep away the wolves, have gone home to their wives, their lives,
their mortgages and their other illusions of safety.

We have no nets. Beer is our high wire; our tightrope.

Drink up please.

See that one there, at the end of the bar,
there's a shadow that's woven itself through all his days,
all his could have beens that never were;
there's a darkness that's woven itself into the very fabric of his being,
there's a hole where his soul should be and nothing could ever fill it.
He defines the word 'insatiable'. Don't we all?

Drink up please.

We are what's left over.
Scraps of people, walking clichés, ordinary statistics in an ordinary world,
the others feed on our misfortune.
It makes them feel better about their own lives,
to see us drowning in each pint of beer.

Drink up please.

Greatness dribbles away. We let it leave.
It exits via the gaps in between our fingers
and we know better than to attempt to clutch at it as it departs.
You might as well clasp at empty air.

Maybe if we'd made it to Finishing School we wouldn't feel so unfinished.
Unmade, incomplete.
Somebody just had his pacemaker fitted.

Heart was beating irregular but now he's back in time, two-four,
and we're all back under the table which is where he drank us to.
Well, we would say, hurry up,
but what is there anyway to hurry up for?
Nothing but it's fine.

It's dark outside but in here there's light.

The captain bailed overboard decades ago, but the ship sails
blithely on.
Are there icebergs? Is there ice?
Yes, we are the ones who forgot to think twice. I'll only say this
one more time.

Drink up please.

Who was it that turned water into wine?
Well, I never saw him don't believe all that shit,
that gliding across the surface of things. We sink.

We're ten truck pile-ups on high speed motorways, we're
decades collapsing into days,
we're full of everybody else's ways, we're all the things that'll
never fit.
We're not really alive, we just resemble it a little bit.

Drink up please.

We're every book you never read,
we're fucked in the heart and we're fucked in the head
we're all the things that are left unsaid,
we may as well be the living dead,
O yeah we're doing fine.

We're what'll be left at the end of time,
we're staccato rhythm and a corny rhyme,
we're all the things you'd never want to find.

Closing time in the pub at the end of the mind.

The Poet Leaves the Table

I've had enough. I quit.
Why should I bother to tell you the truth?

Nobody listens.

Time and again, I enter the dragon's lair,
snatch the pithy, dull, jewels from between his claws
offer them up to a world that is
at best, indifferent, at worst, hostile.

Your time will come.

Oh, *please.* You've all been saying that for decades now.
That's it, that's it, swan past in your chariot, high and mighty,
offering me some titbit of encouragement, a crumb.

Then go off and gorge yourself on that big fat advancement
you got for your latest tome. Did I mention that I myself
offered encouragement to a would-be, unknown, Chinese poet,
working hundred hour weeks in a sweatshop?

He thanked me then spat in my eye. Who could blame him?

Welcome back, dear. There, my dear. O poor Maureen.
Pile on a bit more patronisation.
Nothing will break my spine.
No, there's nothing left to break anymore.

That's it, that's it, do another television interview,
attend another festival, give another book reading/signing,
write another album of songs,
screw a few of your fans. Rape me.
Flash coded signals across the battlefield –
My friend carries the gun,
I'm interested in where the darkness joins the light.

Here, feast your eyes on my bank account.
there's a mortgage there that needs to be paid.
I'm sure it won't make a dint in your millions.

Gather up your minions,
Issue them commands,
drunk on your own power and fame.
Bend over. Let another country kiss your fat arse.

Frankly, I feel fortunate to even own a house.
It wasn't words that bought it. It was slogging it out in the corporate world,
typing up emails, taking dictation, always somebody's bitch
and later, building software, working myself to the ground,
while you all whinged that I had abandoned you,
while sucking back cocktails with your publicists.

I don't mean to sound ungrateful. *Thank you for the music.*

She had been mollycoddled enough.
No, no, I think you mean, she had been *mauled* enough.

This is my letter to a world -
a world that never received it.

Forgive me, children,
me with my two cupped hands,
one full of innocence, one full of blood,
for choosing to leave at the table,
from time to time,
an empty chair.

The Eternal Stupidity of the Wicker Man

Everybody else knew. How could he have been such an idiot?

So naive – *follow us, yoo-hoo, over here, this way, this way, this way to fun.*
That's it, that's it, climb those stairs, one foot after the other, there's quite a view from the top.

Throw away that copy of Jackson's 'The Lottery' you won't be needing that –
don't worry about the orange stuff, sure it looks a bit like flame but it's something else entirely,
orange-coloured air, it won't hurt a bit. Others have been here before you,
you're not the only one. They all climbed down unharmed. Those charred remnants that look a bit like bones are papier mâché and wire painted up pitch black. Don't be fooled by those.

That's it, that's it, step by step, don't look down at the crowd, ignore that voice that yells, "Your suffering is our spectator sport!"
It's only envy. How they'd love to switch places with you.

One is all it takes. There's just no point in asking what you did to deserve it.
You did not choose; you were chosen. All your horses that you declared were Trojan
turned out to be blind and lame. Existence is only a game.
This world is just an illusion, they say – nobody cares what price you pay.

Best to pay nothing, say nothing at all.
Keep your face blank while the stuff they said wasn't flame gets just a little too warm,
it'll all be over soon enough –
in no time at all you'll be gone.

The Fix-It Man

I am the fix-it man.

I am your remedy – I will bring you back from the dead.
I will ease your pain, set you on your feet again.

I speak in clichés, it's true. I could be the death or the birth of you.
I can get you in the door, pick you up off the floor –
O there's nothing I couldn't do for you.

I could put you in jail or grant you release – is your jigsaw missing sky?
I shall find the absent piece.

All the king's horses and all the king's men –
I succeeded where they failed, which is to say,
I'm the guy who put what's-his-face back together again.

I have quite a reputation.

Unformed universes revolve in the palm of my hand.

The Cartographer's Trauma Upon Waking

The lines were there last night, I swear.
Imps must have erased them as I slept.
The blankness that greeted me this morning
was something I failed to foresee.

Everything gone; white out.
My carefully etched countries, not all of them invented,
vanished, as if with a wand.

The unchartered sections also, *here there be monsters* –
which I remember once was penned in my neat calligraphic hand
now reads nothing at all.

No writing on the wall. Or so I thought
until I visited the bathroom and found penned on the inside
of the medicine cabinet door – *Like Sisyphus, you are a sucker.*

Like all who map new territories,
I begin again and again.

The Ghost of Roy Sullivan Laments

Seven times it struck.
Was there something about me that attracted disaster?
I am living proof of some god's malicious streak;
a humble park ranger, singled out.
My torment was their sport – I was the bear that they baited.
A walking exit wound.

Call me paranoid. Somebody up there had it in for me.
Laughing as they swooped by in chariots,
wayward schoolboys with a magnifying glass
on a hot day mutilating an ant.

The first time, in '42, I was up in my tower, on the lookout for fire.
Nothing much was lost – a nail on a toe.

Time two, the summer of '69 – I was knocked right out,
lost my eyebrows, as in some student prank.
Patience was retained – *it's just coincidence.*

The seventies weren't good.

Strike three took place in my own front yard
on home turf (the audacity).
Hair ablaze, I staggered like a drunken Atlas asked to dance,
ignoring the eyes of the neighbours as they peered at me through
net curtains.

The fourth time, alone in the ranger station, my hair set ablaze –
I took to carrying a pitcher of water with me everywhere I went,
in order to put myself out.

Time five, driving in my car, blasted right out –
I hit the road with a thud.

Something snapped inside –
if I saw a cloud I would attempt to outrun it –
but you can't race the weather or the devil. Campground strike;
an ankle bite.

The final blow came as I was angling – I was used to it by then,
went through the hospital doors with a cackle and a shrug.

In the end I took my own life, using my favourite shotgun.
Can you blame me?

Kids, here's the rub –
they say that it was over unrequited love.

Guy Fawkes Gives His Sincerest Apologies

Look guys, I'm all apologies.
I never meant to purchase all that wonderful gunpowder,
never intended to blow your good little government apart.

If I could've, I would've *loved* to have joined you,
a nameless number in a faceless hoarde. I tried; I tried and I failed.
These things happen all the time.
When they sing, they croon not my praises but my crimes.

'Fawkes at midnight, and by torchlight there was found
With long matches and devices underground.'

I was arrogant, of course. Evil little creeps like me always are.
I was something to protect yourself against. Keep me out.
Build a fence. Be sure to ring it with barbed wire.

'O England praise the name of God
That kept thee from this heavy rod!
But though this demon e'er be gone,
His evil now be ours upon!'

I was nothing you should bother with, something that you should keep away from.
An A-bomb. Sooner or later, it's gonna blow. Tragically, it never did though.

Although nothing is for sure, some things are for certain –
I will never grow old, and you can say what you like – *I made history.*

'Remember, remember the 5th of November,
The Gunpowder Treason and plot;
I know of no reason why the Gunpowder Treason
Should ever be forgot.'

I am not dead, only sleeping.

Sunday Evening, Driving West

Drive straight into the setting sun.

The ghosts that shriek around your ears
are just as harmless as flies. Bat them away.
The shackles that they put you in have been broken;
the chains have been changed. Cage door hangs open on its
hinge.
Look up. Orange sky flames bright.

Look neither right nor left. Keep your eyes on the road. Drive.

Drive straight into the setting sun.
Its golden rays will turn you into dust.

Forget the living and the dead;
no-one can touch you here.

You are almost skeletal, your flesh burnt away.
Eyes suspended in a skull. Let the bones of you drive on.

It's all you have to do.
The rest has already been decided for you. Mimic choice.
Raise your voice. Drive on.

It's late Sunday evening and everybody else is sleeping.
The lights in the houses, the factories, are out. Black windows.
Only the street lamps shine. There's nobody else around.

As you vanish behind the far horizon so will the sun,
the two of you going down together, in time, then out of it.

Have fun. The sun will claim what's left of you,
cast no shadow. Leave a mark. Burst into flame.
Rise again – why not? What else have you got planned to do?

Disappear into thin air – the sun will take the best in you, what's old,
drive on into the desert, some god, sizzling, waits for you – devoured without care, without fuss.

You will be nothing, like the rest of us.

You Will Know When You Leave

It is a place of choice. The deep black fissure in the rock
glistens like an open wound. Or some fanged mouth of hell.

You can't even remember what you came here for;
there is no turning back. Dead track.

Down you go, alone, so late,
kelp grasping at your legs like the grubby fingers of ghostly girls.
The bitter salty air stings pores, the seagulls chirp – angelic
lunatics.
The keening wind moans its chorus, your hands cling like
spiders' legs to the walls.

You have no idea where on earth in the world you are.
You are clueless. There are no more planks to break.
Your mind is nothing more nor less than simple blank space.

The ancient songs of extinct birds are blowing in the breeze.
Is there something in or under a rock pool that you think you
might need?
There is no thought here that hasn't been thought before.
There are vampires in the trees.

You won't know when you get there.
You will know when you leave.

Notes

'Ode to Mutt' refers to the Russian space dog Laika. Laika (1954-57) was the first animal to orbit the earth and the first orbital death. The true cause and time of her death was not made public until 2002. It's likely she died from overheating.

'Closing Time in the Pub at the End of the Mind' alludes to T.S. Eliot's *The Waste Land* and to Wallace Stephen's 'The Palm at the End of the Mind'.

'Guy Fawkes Gives His Sincerest Apology' uses quotations from several poems on Guy Fawkes: John Rhodes' narrative verse, John Wilson's 1612 song on the 'gunpowder plot' and the well-known traditional British nursery rhyme.

'The Latest Lighthouse Keeper' alludes to Wallace Stevens's 'Disillusionment of Ten O'Clock.'

'You Will Know When You Leave' references Allen Curnow's poem 'You will know when you get there'.

'Tectonic' alludes to the Elizabeth Bishop poem, 'One Art'. 'Tectonic' refers to the Napier earthquake of 1931 which substantially destroyed large areas of the city. As art deco was popular at the time, a lot of the city's buildings were rebuilt in this style.

Janet Frame, ONZ, CBE, was a New Zealand writer who lived from 1924-2004. Her most well known work is An *Angel at my Table*, an autobiographical novel, which was part of a trilogy, the other two books being *To The Island* and *Envoy to Mirror City*. The trilogy was made into a film called *An Angel at My Table* by Jane Campion in 1990.

Roy Cleveland Sullivan was a U.S. park ranger who worked in Virginia. He was hit by lightning on seven occasions and survived them all. He committed suicide by shooting himself at the age of 71.

From reviews of the first edition of *In Vitro*

I read the book cover to cover in two sittings, my hands gripped the book hard and my eyes were wide a great deal of the time. The poems are so fierce, clean and strong, exhilarating, it felt like I had to hold on tight or fall off.... it's like surgery with a pen.... every single page sings with something like the sound of saw-blades slicing timber... I loved this book.
– Raewyn Alexander, MySpace.

The poems in this collection range across many subjects, from those of day-to-day events such as being locked out of one's home to the extraordinary poems about the Wicker Man, cartographers and Guy Fawkes. Solomon is a tolerant, compassionate observer of nature and human nature. She is able to look into the lives, hearts and minds, not only of people, but of animals – using their thoughts and voices. She is able to draw the reader along with her, as she does in 'Blighty Wounds' and 'The Poet Leaves the Table'. These poems give us vivid glimpses into grief and pain. They are deeply moving. Yet they are not sentimental. Whatever she writes about, Solomon always remains connected with the natural world and is sustained by it; the sense of wonder it inspires shines through her poetry. She used language powerfully to make us experience the world as she does. Together, the poems in this collection form rich form rich and thought-provoking material.
—Patricia Prime, *Takahē* 74 (2011).

This is an accessible volume from a poet who is clearly not up herself, and enjoys communicating with her readers.
—Nicholas Reid, *Landfall*, NZ, July 2011

In Vitro is the debut collection of prize-winning poet, Laura Solomon. ... In just over thirty poems she makes quite a number of bold statements. She hits hard and quickly and offers up plenty of excitement .... if you like your poems with extra muscle, *In Vitro* is the one for you. ... packed with action and laughs. Christopher Morley once said "The courage of the poet is to keep ajar the door that leads into madness." Laura Solomon has begun to open that door in her very first collection.
—Hamesh Wyatt, *Otago Daily Times*, 21 May 2011.

THE INTERNATIONAL PROVERSE PRIZE

Laura Solomon won the inaugural Proverse Prize in 2009 with her novella, *Instant Messages* (Proverse Hong Kong, 2010).

The Proverse Prize, an annual international competition for an unpublished single-author book-length work of fiction, non-fiction, or poetry, the original work of the entrant, submitted in English (translations are welcome) was established in January 2008. It is open to all who are at least eighteen on the date they sign the entry form and without restriction of nationality, residence or citizenship.

Founded by Gillian and Verner Bickley, the objectives of the prize are: to encourage excellence and / or excellence and usefulness in publishable written work in the English Language, which can, in varying degrees, "delight and instruct". Entries are invited from anywhere in the world.

More information, updated from time to time, is available on the Proverse website: proversepublishing.com

Laura Solomon, May 2014.

BOOKS BY LAURA SOLOMON PUBLISHED BY PROVERSE HONG KONG

Brain Graft (2017)
Hilary and David (epistolary novel) (2011). A Proverse Prize Publication.
An Imitation of Life, second revised enlarged edition (novel) (2013).
Freda Kahlo's Cry and Other Poems (2015)
In Vitro (2014)
Instant Messages (novella) (2010). Winner of the inaugural Proverse Prize (2009).
The Shingle Bar Sea Monster and Other Stories (2012).
University Days (2014)
Vera Magpie (2012)

FIND OUT MORE ABOUT OUR AUTHORS, BOOKS, LITERARY PRIZES AND EVENTS

Website: <http://www.proversepublishing.com>.

Proverse Catalogue
downloadable from the website.

Follow us on Twitter
Follow news and conversation: <twitter.com/Proversebooks>.
OR
Copy and paste the following to your browsing window and follow the instructions. https://twitter.com/#!/ProverseBooks

Request our Newsletter
Send your request to info@proversepublishing.com

Availability
Most books are available in Hong Kong and world-wide, as paperbacks (some hardback) and E-books

www.ingramcontent.com/pod-product-compliance
Lightning Source LLC
Chambersburg PA
CBHW051134160426
43195CB00014B/2466